Adam Gondvi

I will take you to the colony of the Chamars and other poems

Translated from Hindi by

Amit Sarwal

Rajmangal Prakashan

An Imprint of **Rajmangal Publishers**

ISBN : 978-9349988385

Published by :

Rajmangal Publishers

Rajmangal Prakashan Building,
1st Street, Ozone, Quarsi, Ramghat Road
Aligarh-202001, (UP) INDIA
Cont. No. +91- 7017993445
www.rajmangalpublishers.com
rajmangalpublishers@gmail.com
sampadak@rajmangalpublishers.in

प्रथम संस्करण : Jan. 2026 – पेपरबैक

प्रकाशक : राजमंगल प्रकाशन

राजमंगल प्रकाशन बिल्डिंग, 1st स्ट्रीट,

ओजोन, क्वार्सी, रामघाट रोड,

अलीगढ़, उप्र. – 202001, भारत

फ़ोन : +91 - 7017993445

First Published : Jan 2026 - Paperback
Printed by : Repro India Ltd.
eBook by : Rajmangal ePublishers (Digital Publishing Division)

Content

Published in collaboration with

Kula Press, Australia

Kula Press, 2 Jetty Road, Werribee South, Victoria 3030,

Australia, E-mail: kulapress@gmail.com /

Website: www.kulapress.com.au

Acknowledgements

I wish to express my sincere gratitude to everyone who made the translation of this book possible.

My heartfelt thanks are due to Dilip Gondvi (poet and nephew of Late Adam Gondvi), Mrs Kamla Devi (wife of Late Adam Gondvi), Alok Kumar (son of Late Adam Gondvi) for permitting me to translate and publish Adam Gondvi's poems from his collection *Samay se mutbhed* ('Encounter with time'; Vani Prakashan, 2010) and *Dharti ki satah par* ('Surface of the earth'; Kitabghar Prakashan, 2012). The views expressed in this work are of Late Adam Gondvi.

I extend my thanks to Prof. Pal Ahluwalia, Prof. Sudesh Mishra, Prof. David Lowe, Prof. David Walker, Assoc. Prof. Shailendra B. Singh, Assoc. Prof. Sakul Kundra, and my colleagues at the University of the South Pacific (USP) and Fiji National University (FNU) for their unwavering support.

I am also deeply grateful to my friends Jitarth Jai Bharadwaj, Pallavi Jain, Prof. Om Prakash Dwivedi, and Assoc. Prof. Sunny Vinnakota for their encouragement throughout this journey.

Special thanks to Dr Urvashi Vashist for her meticulous copy-editing and insightful feedback on my manuscript. I am also sincerely thankful to the publishing teams at Kula Press and Rajmangal Publishers for their professionalism, dedication, and finesse in bringing this project to life.

Lastly, my profound gratitude goes to my wife, Reema Sarwal, and our extended family in India, the USA, Canada, and Germany for their constant belief in my work and their unconditional love.

For Reema, Mishank and Saavi

Introduction

I will take you to the colony of the Chamars and other poems is a collection of seventy-four translated poems originally published as *ghazals*, *nazms* and poems in Hindi and Urdu by Ram Nath Singh 'Adam Gondvi,' the people's poet. Born on 22 October 1947 in a Thakur[1] family to Devkali Singh and Mandvi Singh, Adam Gondvi lived in Gonda, Uttar Pradesh. As the financial situation of the family was poor, he was educated only until class five of the primary school. He spent his entire life working as a farmer on his ancestral land. From childhood, Adam Gondvi was interested in reading poetry. He started attending poetry recitations organized around his village. This resulted in him exploring the avenue of poetry, particularly the *ghazal*, as a vent for suppressed emotions and articulate ideology. He was a man of simple tastes—a white *kurta-payjama*, an *angocha* on his shoulder and black leather shoes were his trademark. And simple ideology—"My self-respect bows down at only two places, / He is either an oppressed or a person of high intellect." Adam Gondvi lived like that until his death. Suffering from liver ailment, he passed away on 18 December 2011 at the Sanjay Gandhi Postgraduate Institute of Medical Sciences in Lucknow, Uttar Pradesh.

In his poetic journey, he published three collections: *Dharti ki satah par* ('Surface of the earth', 1987/2012), *Garam roti ki mahak* ('The Smell of Hot Bread,' 2000), and *Samay se mutbhed* ('Encounter with time,' 2010). A small but very powerful oeuvre from a poet of poverty and

[1] A feudal upper caste.

revolution. During his lifetime, he was known only in the circles of *kavi samelan*[1] but after his death, his revolutionary ideas caught the attention of netizens on social media. This has made him posthumously famous and infamous alike. To understand him, you have to look at his poetry in the context of its social, economic, political and historical milieu. About his own works, Adam Gondvi writes: "On the banks of Sarayu stretched afar, / My poem is the inscription of vivid waves." For his contribution to Hindi and Awadhi, Adam Gondvi was awarded the Dushyant Kumar Prize (1998) by the Madhya Pradesh government and Maati Ratan Samman (2007) by Shaheed Shodha Sansthan. Keeping in mind the subject and style of his poetry, Adam Gondvi would be remembered along with Muktibodh (1917-1964), Dushyant Kumar (1933-1975), Sudama Pandey 'Dhoomil' (1936-1975) and Nagarjun (1911-1998) in the annals of Hindi poetry.

Adam Gondvi was aware that his poetry reflects an awareness of the human predicament in the mechanical age. His poems lack any romantic affectation and literary ornamentation typically synonymous with the writing of the Urdu *ghazal* and *najm*. He defines a poem as: "It is clinging to a vine on the branch of philosophy, / A *ghazal* is the fragrance of jasmine on dewy nights." Although he never defined himself as a *ghazal* writer, Adam Gondvi's style of poetry is very close to Dushyant Kumar's. It must be noted that Dushyant Kumar, being a government employee, was measured in his choice of critical words against the government. Adam Gondvi openly attacks politics,

[1] A formal gathering of poets.

democracy and a system that is rotting away and needs an immediate overhaul. He writes: "Our sovereigns will do what Dalhousie couldn't with the nation, / They'll auction *Hindustan* if you pay a commission."

As a poet, Adam Gondvi used the sharp edge of his pen to give words to the thoughts of the poorest of the poor stuck in the unfair social order. His poems are simple and straight from the heart of a poet who lives in India's everyday reality. At the core, his poems highlight the plight of the oppressed and marginalized such as the women, Muslims and Dalits. He invites you to journey along him and see the plight of Dalits in the villages of India for yourself through the mirror of poetry. He writes: "Come and feel the intense heat of life, / I will take you to the colony of the Chamars. / … I extend an invitation, please come to my village, / Under the shade of mango trees on the banks of rivers, / Villages, where today Panchali is being stripped, / Or where non-violence is being raped." The target of most of his satirical poems are politicians who seek votes from the public in the name of caste, community and nationalism. His poems are a warning to the common people—not to fall in the morass created by corrupt politicians and the heads of religious institutions who have their petty agendas to fulfil. He takes as an example, the 2011 anti-corruption movement and protests held on the banks of river Yamuna in Delhi and writes: "This is the Mahabharata whose characters have arrived, / … Merchants of votes, mantles spread, have arrived." Adam Gondvi didn't just highlight the problems through his poems but in his typical rustic manner also provided solutions to live a meaningful life. For example, look at his advice to the fellow intellectuals and poets of India: "O poets! Return to the skin of the earth, / What are the dawn moon or stars of daybreak but glaze."

To provoke and connect with a larger audience, the people sitting in the back row and the uneducated masses, the language of Adam Gondvi's resistance is Hindustani—a mixture of Urdu, Hindi, Awadhi, English and unsophisticated rustic slang—for his *ghazals*. As a poet, he was a straight shooter: "You say life is *gulmohar* from tip to toe, / In our view, of the poor, life is an atrocity." He spoke plainly to present the everyday lived reality of the common people and used both Hindu and Muslim religious ideas, personas, symbols and beliefs to make his point. He also used popular characters such as from Munshi Premchand and Phanishwar Nath Renu's oeuvre, political figures, couplets, idioms, anecdotes, unconventional subjects and news items to create a base for his original ideas. He writes harshly: "Not from eminence of castles nor the sparkle of runes, / Beau mondes grow lambent in the sweat of Ghisu." He links the themes of spiritual love, elite mannerisms, splendour and the glorification of the beauty of the beloved found in traditional *ghazals* to his protagonists who belong to a different economic stratum, often below the poverty line and uneducated. As a poet, he laments about not writing to the expectations of the elite: "Flowers bloom on an earth of severed breasts, / In my songs might there then be whither from innocence." This shows the depth of poet's understanding of human beings' sufferings and anguish through the realities of village life and daily struggles of the communities on the margins.

It was Adam Gondvi's dream, as reflected through his work, to see a casteless society and equality in India: "I have a dream you must fulfil, / The road from a hut to Rajpath should be invariant." His solution is self-introspection, get rid of materialistic tendencies and start a revolution from villages: "When on the body of democracy there are signs of rape, / People have the right to bear arms and rebel." Although Adam Gondvi, a peasant-poet-thinker, could not bring a revolutionary change in society during his lifetime, his poems would inspire many to strive to create a better world. Given the socio-political conditions of India, Adam Gondvi's poetry that abides by his firm belief in Marxism, will always remain contemporary and teach his message to the coming generations: "We will write a new history of our times."

We will write the pangs of humanity

We will write the pangs of humanity, will write the stench of earth,
We will write a new history of our times.

Silenced for centuries bedecking harems of landlords,
Mudra[1] to Raidass,[2] will write this Dalit tale of woe,

At one end dismissing the art of Premchand,[3]
Sons of Osho[4] will write essays on *Kamasutra*.[5]

Being a destroyer of tradition makes a singular impression,
For them Tulsi[6] is a heretic they will write Derrida[7] as exceptional.

What does the reader have to do with their constrained relationships,
But they are locked in their insistence, they will write self-gratification.

---

[1] Subhash Chandra (1933-2016) also known as Mudrarakshas was an eminent Hindi playwright, journalist, critic and activist.

[2] An Indian mystic poet-saint, social reformer and a spiritual figure of the Bhakti movement during the 15th to 16th century CE.

[3] Munshi Premchand (1880-1936), the pen name of Dhanpat Rai Srivastava, was a Hindi writer famous for his novels such as *Godaan*, *Karmabhoomi*, *Gaban*, *Mansarovar*, and *Idgah*.

[4] Bhagwan Shri Rajneesh (1931-1990), also known as Osho, was a mystic and founder of the Rajneesh movement.

[5] Kamasutra by to Vātsyāyana is an ancient Indian Sanskrit text on sexuality, eroticism and role of emotions in life.

[6] Goswami Tulsidas (1497-1623) was a Ramanandi Vaishnava saint and poet, renowned for his epic *Ramcharitmanas*, a retelling of the Sanskrit Ramayana in Awadhi language.

[7] Jacques Derrida (1930-2004) was an Algerian-born French philosopher known for developing deconstruction.

This is the Mahabharata

This is the *Mahabharata*[1] whose characters have arrived,
When Yoga Guru[2] ran away Anna Hazare[3] arrived.

Whatever Thackeray[4] says Bollywood[5] will repeat,
So in the wings the film stars too arrived.

At the feet of the Baba[6] lies an offshore bank account,[7]
What kind of disciple-folk on the Yamuna's banks arrived.[8]

When Advani[9] and Gadkari[10] came the curtain lifted,
Merchants of votes, mantles spread, have arrived.

---

[1] A Sanskrit epic that narrates the struggle between two groups of cousins, Kaurava and Pandava, in the Kurukshetra War.

[2] Baba Ramdev is an influential yoga guru and co-founder the Patanjali Ayurved Ltd.

[3] A social activist who has led movements to promote government transparency and fight corruption in public life.

[4] Balasaheb Thackeray (1926-2012) was an Indian politician and founder of the Shiv Sena in Maharashtra.

[5] The Indian Hindi-language film industry based in Mumbai, capital of Maharashtra.

[6] See Baba Ramdev.

[7] Black money in offshore banks refers to income earned illegally and not reported to the Indian government so as to avoid paying taxes on it.

[8] The 2011 Indian anti-corruption movement and protests held on the banks of river Yamuna to bring legislation and enforcement against political corruption.

[9] Lal Krishna Advani is an Indian politician and one of the co-founders the Bharatiya Janata Party (BJP).

[10] Nitin Jairam Gadkari is an Indian politician who served as the President of the Bharatiya Janata Party (BJP) from 2009 to 2013.

The pitiful story of the severe flood

The pitiful story of severe flood, renunciation of rivers is written,
On the barks of the old banyan, centuries of history is written.

What kind of game has cruel fate played with her destiny,
On the pages of her mind Shakuntala,[1] and on her lips dismay is written.

The fragrance of dark liqueur, as though at Goswami Tulsi's[2] quatrain,
Yet in dreaming memories, Sita's[3] exile is written.

When gusts of hot loo[4] burn the body,
She has written spring in the desert of my loneliness.

Half-gratification, irresistible passion, this is the truth of human life,
In this chapter of history, the sigh of parting is written.

---

[1] The wife of King Dushyanta and the mother of Emperor Bharata. Her story is told in the *Mahabharata* and Kalidasa in his play *Abhijnanashakuntala.*

[2] Goswami Tulsidas (1497-1623) was a Ramanandi Vaishnava saint and poet, renowned for his epic *Ramcharitmanas*, a retelling of the Sanskrit Ramayana in Awadhi language.

[3] The wife of Lord Ram, King of Ayodhya, who forced into exile two times.

[4] The gusty, hot and dry summer wind.

In whose spell this earth is frenzied

In whose spell this earth is frenzied, the sky too,
This world a riddle, a fable, and history too.

Climbing the steps of contemplation, we come having touched moon and stars,
Yet in the depths of the soul is the musk of earth too.

In which mould will you create the conflict of the human heart,
In the background of great ecstasies, is Osho's[1] retirement too.

As the drops of elixir showered I turned away my head,
Today, I drink poison gladly, I have this awareness too.

We have arrived in this slum crossing the bridge of rainbow,
Where the light of hunger is lovely, sprightly, gallant too.

In this jungle of concrete, flowers blossom sans smell,
In the valleys of memories, you might say, spring is, too.

---

[1] Bhagwan Shri Rajneesh (1931-1990), also known as Osho, was a mystic and founder of the Rajneesh movement.

The Pundit was complaining in the temple today

The Pundit was complaining in the temple today,
A computer will say prayers by the light of kerosene.

There is an error in foreign money minister's junket,
Where the poison of debt mixes in poverty's piece.

The Assembly's temperature rose as Chadaami Lal[1] arrived,
Captive through Emergency,[2] the charge a sugar scam.

---

[1] A persona representing corrupt politicians.

[2] Refers to a 21-month period from 1975 to 1977 when Prime Minister Indira Gandhi declared a state of emergency across India.

Ah! Indignant Hiraman

Ah! Indignant Hiraman,[1] expenses outrage me,
Your New Delhi sees the advent, of post-modernity.[2]

TV, paper, bodies, present desirable cuts,
These our meditations, and our philosophy.

All gods but one God, memorize this, fight it out,
Centuries of struggle acquired us, this sagacity.

Those who were restless to change the system,
Captive in their bungalows be, this nation's majesty.

Leaders walk the walk of Dhritarashtra their laird,[3]
It is the country's shame that you still sit silently.

---

[1] The protagonist of Hindi writer Phanishwar Nath Renu's short story "Maare Gaye Gulfam"

[2] A movement that developed in the mid- to late 20th century across various fields. Defined primarily by an attitude of skepticism, irony, or rejection toward what it describes as the grand narratives and ideologies associated with modernism.

[3] The blind King of the Kuru Kingdom in the epic *Mahabharata*.

This was our momentous, battle against the rich

This was our momentous, battle against the rich,
Where did mosque and *mandir*,[1] come in between?

All over whose face was, written prison walls,
Swathed himself in Ram-Ram,[2] became parliamentary.

To look, to listen tell the truth goes against whose grain,
Sit enthroned on chairs of state, Bapu's three monkeys.[3]

Not to be seen or heard of, even marginally,
Nowadays their faces market every calendar you see.

---

[1] Temple.

[2] Lord Ram is the seventh avatar of the God Vishnu and a king of Ayodhya.

[3] The phrase 'See no evil, hear no evil, speak no evil' adopted as a message of peace and tolerance by Mahatma Gandhi's through the visual metaphor of the three monkeys.

If it rains sex from TV to newspaper

If it rains sex from TV to newspaper,
Tell me how our thinking then do broaden and expand?

Many Alexanders[1] swept away in the flood of time,
How does sense in unbaked clay, the mighty river span?

Civilization strided forth ever fearing death,
China's Great Wall or the Taj's[2] artisan.

My self-regard bowed its head before but two,
He was either an oppressed or a righteous man.

I have a dream you must fulfil,
The road from a hut to Rajpath[3] should be invariant.

---

[1] Alexander the Great was the king of Macedon who created an empire stretching from Greece to northwestern India.

[2] The Taj Mahal is marble mausoleum of Mumtaj Mahal, wife of Mughal Emperor Shah Jahan, on the southern bank of the river Yamuna in Agra.

[3] A ceremonial boulevard in New Delhi (India) that runs from Rashtrapati Bhavan through Vijay Chowk and India Gate to National Stadium.

When creation is in an original peace

When creation is in an original peace,
Conversation happens then between the world and me.

If you ever hear tell, bow your head with grace,
For unexceptionable is the woman's race.

Draw a veil over the horizon, lamps come alight,
Thinking makes it so they say, day may turn to night.

A novel battle is afoot, ideologies engage,
Every day along these lines, anew the check and mate.

Do not invite that solitary man to feast him alone,
Adam[1] arrives in state with a procession of woes.

---

[1] Adam Gondvi.

They think to bloom is to preface the fall

They think to bloom is to preface the fall,
But one's blood must irrigate the garden.

To meet her I must travel many turns,
I have yet to descend to the river of fire.[1]

Whose arrival presages change to the system of the world,
Is yet to arise from these ashes.

The river is flowing, I am parched for a sip,
Mr Uday Pratap Singh,[2] this is breaking your promise.

---

[1] Reference to Mirza Ghalib's couplet.
[2] A noted poet and chairperson of Uttar Pradesh Hindi Sansthaan.

The body is nothing

The body is nothing, have a look at the exposed soul,
Go on, elbow into the crowd and watch this farce too.

Those who can turn the temper of this world's seasons,
Look at dejection writ on the face of youth.

The nation burns and they cajole a race,
Watch the filthy language our eminent Assembly spew.

Matsyagandha[1] will again fall prey to some sage,
The fog and mist spread deep and wide, look.

---

[1] It literally means 'smell of fish.' In the epic *Mahabharata* it is the name of Ved Vyasa's mother, Satyavati. She was the adopted daughter of a fisherman and later the queen of the Kuru king, Shantanu, and the great-grandmother of the Pandava and Kaurava princes. In her youth, Satyavati was seduced by sage Parashara, who fathered her son Vyasa.

Emancipatory consciousness

Emancipatory consciousness, the supplication of history,
This world of the wise is a world of inconsistency.

What you call the golden past in this country's history,
Is the story of mere revenge, fear, and misery.

The old century remained entangled by a demigod's curiosity,[1]
Is this time of anticipation also the time of our thirst?

What has this system given the new generations after all?
The colourfulness of sex or the pills of Salphos.[2]

Remember that ideas just do not mould themselves into a poem,
It matures over slow heat, of feeling.

---

[1] Gondvi refers to 'yaksha prashna'—the phrase is commonly understood among Hindus as the interrogation of Yuddhishthir by Yama, god of death, in the guise of a demigod in the Mahabharata. The interrogation confirms Yuddhishthir's rectitude, wisdom, and vast knowledge. In the story, Yama has interrupted Yuddhishthir as he bent to a lake to quench his thirst.

[2] Aluminium Phosphide is a highly toxic inorganic compound used as a fumigant for stored cereal grains.

Our sovereigns will do what Dalhousie couldn't with the nation

Our sovereigns will do what Dalhousie[1] couldn't with the nation,
They'll auction *Hindustan*[2] if you pay a commission.

Sodden in lust for liquor and lovely ladies,
They'll convert Delhi into Rangila Shah's[3] steam station.[4]

They wake every morning singing Vande Mataram,[5]
But they'll double the price of stuff in market circulation.

If their Assembly seat can be saved with a bribe,
Their next Plan[6] will make paying payoffs tradition.

---

[1] James Andrew Broun-Ramsay, also known as Lord Dalhousie, was the British Governor-General in India (1848-1856).

[2] India.

[3] Nasir-ud-Din Muḥammad Shah (1702-1748) was the Mughal emperor from 1719 to 1748. He was a patron of arts and known by his pen-name was 'Sada Rangila' (Ever Joyous) or 'Muhammad Shah Rangila.'

[4] Turkish bath.

[5] Literally, 'Mother, I bow to thee,' is a poem written by Bankim Chandra Chatterjee in the 1870s. In 1950, the Constituent Assembly of India adopted it as the national song.

[6] The Five-year Plan for economic progress.

If there is an empty pot on the cold stove at home

If there is an empty pot on the cold stove at home,
Tell me how I can write that winter's sunshine is intoxicating.

She roves about our village like a mute beggar,
This February morning is paler than my wife who is ailing.

The lotus of rebellion blooms in my heart's arid river,
When I look, the eyes of children are spilling.

How can I feel again the warmth of this body burning?
The story of my love is a burnt matchstick curling.

Let there be a blindfold on the eyes and a lock on the mind

Let there be a blindfold on the eyes and a lock on the mind,
May my good times remain on top of the mind.

Let Allah bestow me a computer's eyes,
May 'Baba Baltiwala'[1] remain my thinking device.

Let wealth I have, come what may,
May security scams[2] be the news every day.

Adam,[3] what does a public servant want in these lands?
A couple of sycophants, microphone and garlands.

---

[1] Jagdish Prakash Shukla, former Chairman of the City Municipal Corporation, Lucknow.

[2] A reference to Harshad Mehta's 1992 securities scam.

[3] Adam Gondvi.

Those who are not mentioned even in the margins of the Vedas

Those who are not mentioned even in the margins of the *Vedas*,[1]
What have those wretched of the earth do with faith and belief?

Where favours are courted by murdering Shambuka,[2]
What to do with such a system's heinous history?

How regressive the reality we have reaped, this moment,
What shall we do with this downfall, this chokehold, terror and tragedy?

Drought means differently in an intellectual's demesne,
What do with the sensation of sex among the debris?

The smell of warm bread drives us wild,
What make of love's spring, transcendental, otherworldly?

---

[1] The four key texts of Hinduism: the Rigveda, the Yajurveda, the Samaveda and the Atharvaveda.

[2] Shambuka is a *Shudra* (untouchable) ascetic, who is killed by Lord Ram in Valmiki's Ramayana.

Take the ghazal now among spellbinding village views

Take the *ghazal* now among spellbinding village views,
Flair can barely breathe in these urbane academies.

They will possess neither that allure nor perfume nor beauty,
Blooms will blossom, no doubt, among the lawn's long queues.

O poets! Return to the skin of the earth,
What are the dawn moon or stars of daybreak but glaze.

Through intimacy, with incredulity, the poor kept pace,
Passing, they'll change these palace splendors into tombs.

Perhaps the incandescence of starvation has somewhere intensified,
For talk of the bayonet's shade is broadcast, advertised.

Not from eminence of castles nor the sparkle of runes

Not from eminence of castles nor the sparkle of runes,
Beau mondes grow lambent in the sweat of Ghisu.[1]

Now we have bread on the bodice and love on the hem,
The *ghazal* dismounts from the chateau's stairwell.

Literature's mirror passes through those narrow alleys,
Where infancy, whimpering, to the mother's breast cleaves.

This journey till doomsday spans an infinite sea,
They that wish for the shore may climb down the keel.

I have this request of new generations literary,
Cache the legacy of Dhoomil[2] with care, scrupulously.

---

[1] A *Dalit* (untouchable) character from Munshi Premchand's (1880-1936) short story "Kafan" ('The Shroud', 1936).

[2] Renowned Hindi poet Sudama Pandey (1936-1975) who was known for his revolutionary writings and poems published under the pen-name 'Dhoomil.'

Take the feeling of hunger to words and verse

Take the feeling of hunger to words and verse,
Or take words and verse to the world of the destitute.

The *ghazal* intimate now with the beloved's conceits,
Take it to the wrinkles on the widow's brow.

Lecture me later on controlling my verse,
Comport first to grace your very own words.

The water of Ganga[1] is now cultural currency,
Carry this thirst to the swilling of vodka.

People wound themselves per alien deceits,
Carry this city to the vagaries of light.

---

[1] The Ganges, a river worshipped as a goddess in Hinduism and water from the river is sold as a ritual purifier.

The tress – the arch – the smile – the moon – the mirror – the rose

The tress – the arch – the smile – the moon – the mirror – the rose
Their lissomeness sank on the scaffold of starvation

Man is entangled in the geography of hunger
In this era who has leisure to read the book of the heart

Carrying the wound of this century's thirst on our lips
Life is a punishment in this voyage of doubt

Along the vine with religion blossom flowers of riots
Civilization stands unmasked in Rajneesh's[1] *hammam*[2]

Spend a few days in the shade of a footpath
Mister, it is easy to drown in an ocean of scrutiny.

---

[1] Bhagwan Shri Rajneesh (1931-1990), also known as Osho, was a mystic and founder of the Rajneesh movement.
[2] A Turkish bath.

Enmeshed in webs

Enmeshed in webs, in filing cabinets,
How many years till light[1] reaches my village

The old Banyan is witness to how
Rassudhi's hut was lost to the *Sarpanch's*[2] hall

Fields sealed for us were gulped by farms
We receive lease certificates for land, but it lay in the lake

Worthless in this crowded world
Do not mould such coin in this mint, this body.

---

[1] Electricity.

[2] Elected head of the village-level constitutional body of local self-government called the Panchayat.

The moon lies underfoot

The moon lies underfoot, the sun is a toy,
Yes and character in this age is a dwarf.

Whenever homes of paupers burned in city riots,
The view from bungalow lawns became pretty.

Man carries his coffin on his shoulders,
While the meaning of life has become an unbearable burden.

Even Adam[1] had coverings of leaves,
As the soul became naked, the weather turned hideous.

No Layla[2] pledges her love any longer,
In this age, the symbol of love has become triangular.

---

[1] Adam and Eve.

[2] Layla-Majnun is an old Arabic story about the 7th-century Najdi Bedouin poet Qays ibn al-Mullawah and his ladylove Layla bint Mahdi.

It is either a hostage of starvation or under the shadow of the gallows

It is either a hostage of starvation or under the shadow of the gallows,
My beloved India is under the shade of a sword.

The sunlight of despair has swept across the mulch of the mind,
Man is under the shade of a falling wall.

An ocean of helplessness is spread afar,
And our paper boat is under the shade of an oar.

Don't ask about the tranquillity of us *fakirs*,[1]
Which is under the shade of your wavy tresses.

---

[1] A Muslim or Sufi religious ascetic who lives solely on alms.

Shall we call it hunger of the body or fever of lust

Shall we call it hunger of the body or fever of lust,
It is not appropriate to call superficial emotion – love

What the endowment of an individual has often swung aside,
How shall we call it the momentum of time.

The air is heavy with the stench of man on fire,
Yet an obstinate insistence the weather be referred to as fine

Armstrong[1] says that the moon is a rock,
In these present times, what shall we call touchstone of beauty.

---

[1] Neil Armstrong (1930-2012) was an American astronaut and the first person to walk on the Moon.

A man does not sell his integrity just like that

A man does not sell his integrity just like that,
Hunger takes a person to that turn in the road.

Endurance has a limit – please pay attention,
Till when do we keep the *dastarkhan*[1] warm on supplicating slogans?

The warmth of moist lips will not satiate,
The man enmeshed in the geography of hunger.

It is utter folly to say civilization in this age
Will be able to transverse a desert of hatred.

---

[1] Turkish word for tablecloth.

She of the blistered hands and chapped feet

She of the blistered hands and chapped feet –
Because of her brilliance arrived at your bungalow.

Here, the average of a day's income is a quarter,
There, earnings of Gandhi's[1] followers run in lakhs.[2]

Any loon may rape her with a threat,
In this sense our country is the idiot's wife.

How costly this bread that woman will tell,
Who pawned her body to pay for it.

---

[1] Mohandas Karamchand Gandhi (1869-1948) was a lawyer and a non-violent anti-colonial nationalist who has inspired movements for civil rights and freedom across the world.

[2] A lakh (Lac or Lacs) is a unit in the Indian numbering system equal to one hundred thousand (100,000).

Till when shall we bear the tyranny of friends and enemies?

Till when shall we bear the tyranny of friends and enemies?
The tears of the poor will be moulded now in flame.

On one hand are we, burning in the hell of the starvation,
On the other are you, repeating fortune tales.

Since the dusk of famine descended on the village,
All close relationships were rendered meaningless.

Pen in one hand and hoe in the other,
The writer's dreams are rooted in the soil.

One unsuccessful in some apparent love in this world

One unsuccessful in some apparent love in this world,
Is a Rousseau,[1] a Hitler,[2] a Khayyam.[3]

We either poison him or take him to the guillotine,
This is the end of a Mansour[4] in these times.

By all means, if one wants to embrace in a frenzy of desire one may,
There is a missive on the wind from the beloved somewhere.

Often in the corridors of power at a sign from Zulaikha,[5]
The reality is, Yusuf[6] is auctioned, still.

---

[1] Jean-Jacques Rousseau (1712-1778) was a Genevan philosopher, writer and composer.

[2] Adolf Hitler (1889-1945) was a German politician and leader (Fuhrer) of the Nazi Party responsible for the genocide of the Jews.

[3] Omar Khayyam (1048-1131) was a Persian mathematician, astronomer, philosopher, and poet.

[4] Mansour Hallaj (c. 858-922) was a Persian mystic, poet and teacher of Sufism. Condemned and beheaded for heresy.

[5] The wife of Potiphar, the captain of Pharaoh's guard. According to the Book of Genesis, she falsely accused Yusuf (Joseph) of attempted rape after he rejected her sexual advances.

[6] Yusuf (Joseph) was sold into slavery to Potiphar by his jealous brothers.

With a mere salary dispatch what caprices of the wife

With a mere salary dispatch what caprices of the wife,
Mr Sinha has a thousand ways to make money.

Look at this souvenir of drought in his living room,
That new TV set stood on the tripod.

That tinkle inopportunely in Mrs Sinha's hands,
These bangles on her wrist are the gift of the last flood.

Who knows what these sons of Macaulay[1] think of themselves as,
We are Tharu before them, of Terai.[2]

I have sketched an image of Mother India thus,
A helpless cow is tied to the picket of a butcher.

---

[1] Thomas Babington Macaulay (1800-1859) was a British historian and politician. In 1835, he published his argument on the subject of introducing English language in Indian school to create a class of 'brown sahibs.'

[2] Tharu people are an ethnic group indigenous to the Terai in southern Nepal and northern India.

Bearing in mind starvation, unemployment, and smuggling

Bearing in mind starvation, unemployment, and smuggling,
Let us offer the year '87 up to communal riots.

Friend! Go visit the fatherland at Maliyana,[1]
This government of the people is two steps ahead of Hitler.[2]

To pass the night is arduous here, for slow starvation,
There, the evening dances, in a bottle of scotch.

Adam,[3] the wheat farmers will grow bombs instead,
You may deliver our message to the regime.

---

[1] Maliyana is on the outskirts of Meerut city in Uttar Pradesh. Here, in 1987, 72 Muslims were killed in communal violence allegedly by the members of the Provincial Armed Constabulary (PAC).

[2] Adolf Hitler (1889-1945) was a German politician and leader (Fuhrer) of the Nazi Party responsible for the genocide of the Jews.

[3] Adam Gondvi.

The weather of the village is rosy in your files

The weather of the village is rosy in your files,
But these statistics are false, this averment bookish lies.

There, they beat the drums of democracy,
Here, behind the *purdah*[1] is barbarity and *nawabi*.[2]

There is a kind of fighting between wealth and poverty,
This is capitalism's fundamental, structural malady.

Your tables are made of silver and your goblet of gold,
Here the plate is broken even now at Jumman's[3] home.

---

[1] Curtain. The word also refers to the face covering worn by women, and to the practice of sequestering them within the domestic space, ostensibly to preserve their modesty.

[2] Feudalism, from the word 'nawab' (anglicized as 'nabob' during British rule), a word referring to an aristocrat, in increasingly derogatory terms through modern Indian history.

[3] May refer to a common Muslim man or a character Jumman Sheikh from Premchand's short story "Panch Parmeshwar" ('The Holy Panchayat").

Who could have hoped when the light grew nubile

Who could have hoped when the light grew nubile,
She would be kind to the darkness maligned.

From city to city contention of tongue and tongue,
I feel the next extraction will be untongued.

Flowers bloom on an earth of severed breasts,
In my songs might there then be whither from innocence.

Come sometime to the village assembly,
I may be or may not be, but hunger hosts surely.

If a handful of historical records you alter

If a handful of historical records you alter,
Will you thereby change the fate of a race?

Point-counterpoint that emerge from the verse of Raskhan,[1]
Will you change that alluring portrait of Krishna?

From Jayasi[2] this river of Hindi came coursing,
Will you turn its course or the water alter?

Is the truth true by Deshmukh's[3] word, Authorities,
Will you change the interpretation of Mumtaz's dreams?

History tells us that you too are a raider,
Will you revise the robbery of Dravidian[4] estates?

---

[1] Syed Ibrahim Khan 'Raskhan' (1548-1628) was a poet of Pashtun origins, who became a devotee of Lord Krishna.

[2] Malik Muhammad Jayasi (1477-1542) was a Sufi poet. He is known for the epic poem Padmavat (1540).

[3] Nanaji Deshmukh (1916-2010), leader of the Bharatiya Jan Sangh.

[4] 'Dravidian' refers to cultures now primarily located in south India.

Do not paw at Hindu or Muslim sensibilities

Do not paw at Hindu or Muslim sensibilities,
Do not pick at passions for your seat.

Some one among us is a Hun,[1] is a Shaka,[2] is a Mongol,[3]
Do not finger a buried matter any longer.

If the mistakes were Babur's,[4] why should Jumman's[5] house smoke?
Do not, in such fragile times, vex the status quo.

Where are Hitler,[6] Halagu,[7] the Tsar[8] or Genghis Khan,[9]
All vanished now – do not touch on the competence of a clan.

Pull together to trigger war against poverty,
Friend do not dis my devotional poetry.

---

[1] The Huns were a nomadic people who lived in Central Asia, the Caucasus, and Eastern Europe between the 4th and 6th century AD.

[2] Indo-Scythians (also called Indo-Sakas) were a group of nomadic Iranian peoples who migrated southward into western and northern South Asia from the middle of the 2nd century BC to the 4th century AD.

[3] The Mongols are an East Asian ethnic group native to Mongolia and to China's Inner Mongolia Autonomous Region.

[4] Zahīr ud-Dīn Muhammad (1483-1530) was the founder of the Mughal Empire and first Emperor of the Mughal dynasty (r. 1526–1530) in the Indian subcontinent.

[5] May refer to a common Muslim man or a character Jumman Sheikh from Premchand's short story "Panch Parmeshwar" ('The Holy Panchayat").

[6] Adolf Hitler (1889-1945) was a German politician and leader (Fuhrer) of the Nazi Party responsible for the genocide of the Jews.

[7] Hulagu Khan (c. 1215-1265) was the grandson of Genghis Khan. He conquered much of Western Asia.

[8] Tsar was a title used to designate East and South Slavic monarchs or supreme rulers of Eastern Europe.

[9] Genghis Khan (c. 1155/1162-1227) was the founder and Emperor of the Mongol Empire.

You say life is gulmohar from tip to toe

You say life is *gulmohar*[1] from tip to toe,
In our view, of the poor, life is an atrocity.

Honor's vine has wilted in the glare of starvation,
Life is more acrid than the spasm of death.

Flowers of riots bloom interminably on religion's bough,
In the shade of a dream life is still oblivious.

Until now you went on fornicating with the corpse of light,
Nursing the delusion that life is the sun and the moon.

The point where the new generation's love gets buried,
Life is that filthy gutter along the alleyways of the city.

---

[1] Delonix regia, also known as the flame of the forest, is a flowering tree common to south Asia. It bears cascades of flamboyant red-orange flowers, and is symbolic of opulent and fertile beauty.

Roasted cashews on the plate and whiskey in a glass

Roasted cashews on the plate and whiskey in a glass,
Ram *raj*[1] has descended on the assemblyman's villa.

They are *pukka* Socialists – be they smugglers or dacoits,
Such is the effect of bright *khadi*[2] attire.

How do those observe the celebration of independence
Who arrived on the footpath in search of a home.

With money you might topple a government if you wished,
Parliament has changed at the chattel market.

The people have one choice only – mutiny,
I say this in full possession of mental faculties.

---

[1] Literally, the rule of Ram - signifying an ascent of peace and plenty. Ram is the hero of the Hindu epic Ramayana, a prince who self-exiles to discharge his filial duty and vanquishes all evil. He is an avatar of Vishnu, the divine preserver, is the mythical epitome of integrity and valour, and the perpetually imminent renewal of his reign has become a contemporary symbol of Hindutva's triumph.
[2] A hand-woven natural fibre cloth. Popularized by Gandhi during the independence movement as a homespun alternative to British cotton.

Nagarjun is the exposition of the Leftist thought

Nagarjun[1] is the exposition of leftist thought,
Nagarjun is a synonym for faith in this life.

Creations redolent with the pastoral, and with the pride of the weaver,[2]
Nagarjun is as pleasurable as he is pioneering.

Oh, we say Nagarjun is Bengal's[3] pristine morning,
Kerala's[4] beautiful evening is Nagarjun.

He is so special his existence is a benefaction,
Nagarjun is a regular in the shacks of the poor too.

Along with this era Yazid[5] will lose,
Nagarjun is the herald of the Battle of Karbala.[6]

---

[1] Nagarjun (1911-1998) was a well-known known Hindi and Maithili poet and writer.

[2] Reference to the 15th century mystic Kabir, a weaver by profession, Muslim by birth, who composed exceptonal, supra-devotional poetry influenced by his Hindu Vaishnavite teacher Sant Ramananda critiquing egotism and dogmatc thought, and inspiring a distinct, inclusive, egalitarian, and empathic strand of Indian philosophy.

[3] A state in eastern India.

[4] A state on India's tropical Malabar Coast.

[5] Yazid ibn Mu'awiya ibn Abi Sufyan (646-683) was the second caliph of the Umayyad caliphate. His caliphate was marked by the death of Prophet Muhammad's grandson Husayn ibn Ali.

[6] It was fought on 10 October 680 between the armies led by Yazid I and Husayn ibn Ali.

Whichever way you cast your eyes is the terror of the deluge

Whichever way you cast your eyes is the terror of the deluge,
Trees drowned in the flood and the sky dark-blue.

The one left tangled in the bushes before me,
Is the corpse of a drowned human being.

Snakes are wrapped around the babul's[1] thorny stature,
To what an extent these loons have faith in life.

How savage are the chaste banks of Sarayu,[2]
The waves leap metres in anticipation of the apocalypse.

It is common knowledge that man has defeated nature,
The secret of human might is here manifest.

---

[1] Also known as a gum Arabic tree.
[2] A river that originates in Uttarakhand and flows through Uttar Pradesh.

My poem is a portrait of Asian beauty

My poem is a portrait of Asian beauty,
My poem is a new construction in the Oriental craft.

Nurtured for years in sight of Heer-Ranjha,[1]
My poem is an expression of that golden dream.

Time's hands could not denude its immaculacy,
Think of my poem as the raiment of Draupadi.[2]

Look, with her glass heart she ran into a convergence,
My poem is a sword, in a petal's likeness.

How to describe the animation of a village water-well?
My poem is desolate in the glaring heat of starvation.

O, Adam![3] On the banks of Sarayu[4] stretched afar,
My poem is the inscription of vivid waves.

---

[1] A popular Punjabi tragic romance tale about Heer Syal and Dheedo Ranjha written by Sufi poet Waris Shah (1722-1798) in 1766.

[2] The wife of the five Pandavas in the epic *Mahabharata*. After the game of dice, she was dragged by the hair to the court and is called a whore. The Kauravas make an attempt to disrobe her but she is miraculously protected by Lord Krishna.

[3] Adam Gondvi.

[4] A river that originates in Uttarakhand and flows through Uttar Pradesh.

All the bastards close as husk to the maize

All the bastards close as husk to the maize,
Have come as headmen to the next lane.

Those who had a record of scaling walls,
They have become chieftain in the ebb of age.

As licence to counterfeiters was disbursed pronto,
Whatever riverland had remained unengaged.

The barren land you see fit to lease dearly,
Are pieces of bread when the fever rages.

When a ten-minute prayer lasts hour after hour,
Know an indigent has been hunted like prey.

Nilofer, speak not of dew but of the spark

Nilofer, speak not of dew but of the spark,
Talk about time's altered measure and mark.

Steam does not rise of water warm in moderation,
Speak of ammunition to bring revolution.

Since we can't all adore our celestial begetter,
Talk about some worldly, earth-dwelling character.

A people might perish from forswearing self-reflection,
Abeyance is a crime, speak now of acceleration.

First, Sir, toss up some prodigious slam

First, Sir, toss up some prodigious slam,
Then round the social neck the load of levy ram.

Where folk may be exacting bribes as their due,
Is there another country, its case introduce.

A woman is like the shoe on your foot,
Whenever you feel bored give her the boot.

There is no sugar at home and, oh, we have guests,
On the hearth of rising prices boil straightforwardness.

From palace to hut, a suffocating sadness

From palace to hut, a suffocating sadness,
Someone's stomach is empty, someone's soul is athirst.

To burn someone's home in fealty to God,
This religious loyalty is in fact power-play.

That the back is exposed when we cover the front,
My share of freedom is in a pauper's begging bowl.

The torridity of speeches could never light a stove,
The regime is brazen in this here jungle of vows.

Our village Gobar[1] is in your Lucknow,
Write in an answering letter which hood he's inhabitant of.

---

[1] Literally, cowdung. Gobar is the name of a character in Munshi Premchand's classic novel, Godaan (1936). He typifies the aspirational migrant.

They claim the poor's rally succeeded

They claim the poor's rally succeeded,
But the truth is, the weather worsened.

But yesterday they stopped forced labour in the chieftain's fields,
The very next day another Hori[1] was dispossessed.

When someone's honour was auctioned in a brothel,
Once again Ahalya's[2] body turned from head to foot to stone.

Glossed over in colour and unction, this aspect has no heart within,
Today's human being too has become a figure of paper.

Forgive me, if I tell you the truth, in today's Hindustan,
Only the womb is fertile, feeling has become barren.

---

[1] Hori, a righteous peasant, is the central character in the novel *Godaan* ('Cow donation'; 1936) written by Munshi Premchand (1880-1936).

[2] The wife of the sage Gautama Maharishi who was seduced and raped by Lord Indra. She was cursed to become a stone by her husband.

While seventy of a hundred people are at present wretched, dreary

While seventy of a hundred people are at present wretched, dreary,
Can you say hand on heart this country is free.

Don't measure the value of a country by its stately homes,
The real Hindustan is peopled on the sides of roads.

In the city where the stage managers are blind,
In that city talking about light is futile.

It is up to the next generation, they must judge
Whether reverence for Gandhi[1] or Naxalism is apt and just[2]

This poem is dedicated to the late Manto, my friends,[3]
In whose fiction is a reckoning of cold flesh.[4]

---

[1] Mohandas Karamchand Gandhi (1869-1948) was a lawyer and a non-violent anti-colonial nationalist who has inspired movements for civil rights and freedom across the world.

[2] The term Naxal derives from the name of the village Naxalbari in West Bengal, where the Naxalite peasant revolt took place in 1967. It is now considered a legacy of the Communist Party of India (Marxist–Leninist) founded in Calcutta in 1969.

[3] Saadat Hasan Manto (1912-1955) was a well-known Urdu writer and playwright.

[4] "Thanda Gosht" ('Cold Flesh'; 1950) is a short story written by Saadat Hasan Manto. He was charged with obscenity for this story and faced a trial in criminal court in Pakistan.

Oh God plagued by what obsession are people

Oh God Plagued by what obsession are people,
Drenched in the blood of their kin are people.

This longing is witness that wounded their soul,
Bedecked with a sweet smile on the countenance people.

Ruth expired so man died, in truth,
Rites of life, alone, discharging, people.

For saying so saying happy may the new year be,
Hiding too a dagger in the sleeve, people.

Life is hard

Life is hard, uff, at this inflation, look,
And then at our leaders' fiery speeches, look.

Bearing a begging bowl they urge going to the moon,
This coquetry, this naivety, this gasconade, look.

May the country go to hell, they do not care,
They are clinging to the chair, their exertions, look.

Friends! What other insult can be offered the beard?

Friends! What other insult can be offered the beard?
The consciousness of Rajneesh[1] hooked to the brasserie.

Whether or not the convolutions of yoga achieve resolution,
You have all achieved familiarity with the face of Iblis.[2]

Reverend gentleman with one foot in the grave,
Desires a girl of some sixteen, some nineteen.

In the light of his philosophy, the soul stands naked,
Why don't the faculties now ascend to an investigation?

In the valley of the body divine revelation sought,
By Kore[3] village's Jagdish[4] this repulsive addiction got of.

---

[1] Bhagwan Shri Rajneesh (1931-1990), also known as Osho, was a mystic and founder of the Rajneesh movement.

[2] Iblis is the figure of the devil (*shaitan*) in the Quran.

[3] Name of the village Osho initially established his ashram in. In Hindi the name means 'blank' or 'virgin.'

[4] Literally, 'Lord of the World'. Mockingly signifies 'god' while rhyming with Osho's given name.

We are the last castes Koris and Pasis

We are the last castes[1] *Koris*[2] and *Pasis*,[3]
Because we are inhabitants of India.

Should we search for ourselves in the *Vedas*?[4]
Do we believe in ideality.

Touching our shadow is an accursed act,
We are such annihilators.

Let the of contractors of religion say,
Which planet are we the tribes of.

---

[1] Fourth of four castes in Hinduism - commonly considered untouchable.
[2] A lower caste of weavers.
[3] A Dalit community whose main traditional occupation is tapping toddy.
[4] The four key texts of Hinduism: the Rigveda, the Yajurveda, the Samaveda and the Atharvaveda.

Udaypratap's conduct is like that of a Fakir

His thought is like Ghalib's[1] but the lineage is Mir's,[2]
Udaypratap's[3] conduct is like that of a *Fakir*.[4]

Year after year, he has kept the light of literature alive,
By carrying the burden of the grief of thousands of poor people,
His thoughts mould into poems like this,
As though the flowers of a vine are bathed in morning dew.
He has the joviality of Rang[5] and leisure of Nazeer,[6]
Udaypratap's conduct is like that of a *Fakir*.

He is so friendly a get together goes on late into the night,
In the red glass, even Himalaya's[7] ice will ease,
When friends are with you the milieu is amazing,
With the warmth of tranquillity, even the heart will melt.
In the elite circles of Delhi what awe commands this *Ahir*,[8]
Udaypratap's conduct is just like that of a *Fakir*.

He moulded Roopmati's[9] folktale into verse,

---

[1] Mirza Ghalib (1797-1869) was a popular poet.

[2] Mir Muhammad Taqi Mir (1723-1810) was one of the pioneers of Urdu poetry.

[3] Uday Pratap Singh (1932-) is a politician, poet and chairperson of Uttar Pradesh Hindi Sansthaan. For his contribution to Hindi, he has been recognised with a Sahitya Shiromani award.

[4] A religious ascetic.

[5] Muḥammad Shah (1702-1748) was Mughal emperor from 1719 to 1748 and wrote under the pen-name of *Sada Rangila* (Ever Joyous).

[6] Nazeer Akbarabadi (1735-1830) was a poet known as 'Father of Nazm.'

[7] A mountain range separating the plains of the Indian subcontinent from the Tibetan Plateau.

[8] The Yadav community.

[9] Queen Roopmati was a poet and the consort of Baz Bahadur, the Sultan of Malwa.

Asked the neighbouring country[1] a fiery question,
Quietly the moonlight came and sat in bed,
Very skillfully, he tossed the heart like a coin for tail or heads.
Of our era is this miracle is of the *Pir*,[2]
Udaypratap's conduct is just like that of a *Fakir*.

The one who crossed the river in an old boat,
The one who bravely attacked the burning questions,
There are so many prickles on Socialism's the path,
SO he gave a new edge to the Hindi *Ghazal*.[3]
It is not just hollow verbosity but a decision of integrity,
Udaypratap's conduct is like that of a *Fakir*.

While living in Delhi he has seen the leisure of the rich,
While living abroad he has seen the human flesh market,
May he be Buddhinath,[4] Neeraj,[5] or Nirdhan,[6]
He has seen so many bathing warfs with Som.[7]
However, Uday's passionless heart is like that of Kabir,[8]
Udaypratap's conduct is like that of a *Fakir*.

People say there is dishonesty in politics,
He knows how much water flows in Yamuna,[9]
Declining to go with his mind wherever he listened to his heart,
There alone the colour of this poet's verses are light green.

---

[1] Pakistan.
[2] A Sufi saint.
[3] Poetry.
[4] Buddhinath Mishra (1949-) is a poet and writer based in Bihar.
[5] Gopaldas 'Neeraj' (1924-2018) was a popular poet and author. He was awarded the Padma Shri in 1991 and Padma Bhushan in 2007 by the Government of India.
[6] Shishupal Singh 'Nirdhan' was a Hindi and Urdu poet.
[7] Som Thakur (1934-) is a well-known poet of Brajbhasha and lyricist of Hindi film songs.
[8] Kabir Das was a 15th-century Indian mystic poet and saint.
[9] The second-largest tributary river of the Ganga.

Listen carefully, as this elegy is that of Dabeer,[1]
Udaypratap's conduct is like that of a *Fakir*.

[1] Mirza Salaamat Ali Dabeer (1803-1875) was an Urdu poet who excelled and perfected the art of *marsiya* writing (religious elegiac poems).

We have neither electricity nor water, only potholes on the road

We have neither electricity nor water, only potholes on the road,
Look how beautiful is the atmosphere of our city, Gonda![1]

Come here and see the feudalistic swagger of our district someday,
It is said that in Uttar Pradesh[2] there is no king or queen.

We do not have a place to stay but will build a house for Lord Ram,[3]
Call it magic or you can just call it pompous talk.

We auction morality weighing it in kilograms,
Nevertheless it is our vow that we have to save our honour.

Robbery-Murder-Riot, all are done in the name of saving religion,
In our deeds discernable the flow of Sarayu River.[4]

The one from whom the fragrance of Buddha's character comes,
It is the same people's agony told by the poet's tongue.

---

[1] Gonda district is situated 120 km northeast of Uttar Pradesh's state capital Lucknow.
[2] A state of India.
[3] Refers to the building of Ram Temple in Ayodhya (Uttar Pradesh). The Hindus consider this site as the birthplace of Lord Ram (Ram Janmabhoomi).
[4] A river that originates in Uttarakhand and flows through Uttar Pradesh.

Let the difficulty remain placed like this in the path of life

Let the difficulty remain placed like this in the path of life,
This thirsty longing should continue to doomsday.

The rulers have drawn a line on canvas,
Say circumscribed by its border creativity must stay.

Let the country go to hell, they do not care,
They only have one worry: that their family keep its reign.

Commoners become conservatives in that atmosphere,
Where the shadow of fear lies heavy on feeling.

By the heat of which blossom the roses of revolution,
Safe in your bosom let that spark stay.

The colour of someone is grass green, some are coloured yellow

The colour of someone is grass green, some are coloured yellow,
The bevy of our writers is split into blocs.

My friends, till far away along the horizon there is no shadow of a cloud,
How is the hem of their opinions wet?

That Taj Mahal[1] they call the pillar of beauty,
Here in the eyes of Ghisu[2] it is but a mound of stone.

I hope Adam[3] they will be denuded by a gust of westerly wind,
The skirt of our national culture is so loose.

---

[1] An ivory-white marble mausoleum on the bank of Yamuna River in Agra. It was commissioned by the Mughal emperor Shah Jahan to house the tomb of his wife, Mumtaz Mahal.
[2] A *dalit* character from Munshi Premchand's (1880-1936) story "Kafan" ('The shroud', 1936).
[3] Adam Gondvi.

By putting a lock on our tongue

By putting a lock on our tongue,
You will not be able to cage the flight of our thoughts.

Bungalows will be constructed for pet dogs,
You and I will keep yearning for a home.

So long as there are lackeys of the rich in the community,
The peasant is not fated to feel happiness.

If you count your fingers at home they are no less than claws,
You hang the triangular mark[1] on the office wall.

---

[1] Refers to the Indian Standards Bureau mark on certified gold.

In the river of pain

In the river of pain, a *ghazal* is the flow of tears,
A *ghazal* is an endless play of natural beauty.

It is clinging to a vine on the branch of philosophy,
A *ghazal* is the fragrance of jasmine[1] on dewy nights.

The civilization on the Nile[2] was washed away by the waves of Ganga,[3]
A *ghazal* like unalloyed Hindi is Hindu[4] from head to toe.

If Jafri[5] is searching for Marxist headlines,
A *ghazal* is saffron in the eyes of Bekal Utsahi.[6]

No doubt she was familiar with the tinkling sound of the wine decanter,
A *ghazal* is now a representative of the experience of life.

The character of which is irreplaceable in Asia, Adam,[7]
The *ghazal* is a pure gift from Mirza Ghalib.[8]

---

[1] Night-blooming Jasmine (*Cestrum nocturnum*).
[2] River Nile.
[3] River Ganges.
[4] The word Gondvi uses is 'hinduani' - female Hindu. English does not use the same universal binary gendering of nouns - the image of the ghazal as a Hindu (woman) is practically untranslatable.
[5] Ali Sardar Jafri (1913-2000) was a writer, poet, critic and film lyricist.
[6] Padma Shri Muhammad Shafi Ali Khan (1924-2016), popularly known as 'Bekal Utsahi,' was a poet, writer and politician.
[7] Adam Gondvi.
[8] Mirza Ghalib (1797-1869) was a popular Urdu poet.

If this splendid evening of spring were spent fasting

If this splendid evening of spring were spent fasting,
My assertion is that the magic of its beauty would fade.

I sat down to sketch the contour of your face in my thoughts,
I was surprised to see that the image of bread appeared.

Someday should a ray of joy erupt on the lips of the poor,
Till doomsday should that moment stay still in my poems.

If they spent just one night in the courtyard of a slum,
Rich people's allusion of beautiful dreams would scatter.

If we separate the share of other races from this,
The veil of civilization from India will drop.

Everyone has at least two villages

Everyone has at least two villages,
But only one in a million has an eye to see sorrow.

Do not accuse me of promoting naked words,
The distasteful truth is without clothes.

What kind of impoverishment is this of modern thought?
They search for creativity in the mould of religion.

How helpless are those sleeping on the footpath?
Even animals and birds are in search of a home.

The truth is bound within courteous institutions, but,
The distinct style of a village has its own sweetness.

Let us disrobe the spell of relationships

Let us disrobe the spell of relationships,
Let us gossip about modern creativity.

Those who have been mugged in the light of the day many times,
They will search for darkness in the light.

I am not one to show the path to those who are lost,
What right have we to merely spit on the world?

Those who received contentment from wealth and riches,
Mate, arrange me with that person a face-to-face.

Adam,[1] with what heart call them a good gardener,
Who auctions the colours and fragrance of their garden.

[1] Adam Gondvi.

It has the fragility of flowers and hardness of a cliff

It has the fragility of flowers and hardness of a cliff,
Language is a weaver's[1] thread stretched on a bow.

Come on, let us here hold onto the hem of wisdom,
It is murderous as the steep slope of a mountain.

Scared of it be the caretakers of creativity,
She is collecting her dues like a Pathan.[2]

When the country was sleeping in the lap of enmity,
She was raised in that moment like the prayer of *Azan*.[3]

How can you separate a thorn from a flower?
She came down on abuses like a rustic peasant.

---

[1] Refers to Kabir who belonged to weaver community.
[2] The Afghan henchman of a loan shark.
[3] The Islamic call to prayer.

Friends, that which showers fire from the edge of the horizon

Friends, that which showers fire from the edge of the horizon,
So many hopes were tied to that splendid dawn.

Under the mask of restraint, all look civilized,
If you look in the context of a mob, they look like cannibals.

We had come to the city for the dispersal of beastliness,
To be denuded, from the jungles.

Today, its thrashing cannot be expressed,
The screams of human beings are drowned by the noise of machines.

In the mirror of the word, time's image is pointillate,
Truth acceded to respect by the poetic imagination.

Carrying our own corpse like this on our shoulders

Carrying our own corpse like this on our shoulders,
Hey! People of the city, we have come from villages.

The redness of my blood is in the flowers of your lawns,
Why are you hiding the truth like this.

In nakedness, we are not behind you,
You are naked as a hobby and we are suffering in sorrow.

Look at Rousseau,[1] do not go on Khayyam,[2]
Storms have come of flowers of words too.

---

[1] Jean-Jacques Rousseau (1712-1778) was a Genevan philosopher, writer and composer.

[2] Omar Khayyam (1048-1131) was a Persian mathematician, astronomer, philosopher, and poet.

The composition is fragrant in the colours of the rainbow

The composition is fragrant in the colours of the rainbow,
The poetry of Amrita[1] is a living portrait.

The bitterness of broken relationships is in your verses,
Truly, this is the effect of the soil of Punjab.[2]

The sharp pierce of love's failure torments our hearts,
As though truly the tale of Heer[3] from dewy lips.

The woman who often received infamy in this world,
In your poems, she is not a petal but a sword.

From Gangajal[4] to Vodka this journey, Adam,[5]
In the institutions of Punjabi literature is a new creation.

---

[1] Amrita Pritam (1919-2005) was a Punjabi novelist, essayist and poet.
[2] A state of India.
[3] A popular Punjabi tragic romance tale about Heer Syal and Dheedo Ranjha written by Sufi poet Waris Shah (1722-1798) in 1766.
[4] The holy water of River Ganges.
[5] Adam Gondvi.

Keep every successive experience of tyranny sharp

Keep every successive experience of tyranny sharp,
So that people will forget the history of Changez.[1]

To give a gift to coming generations,
Display the corpse of humanity in the showcase.

Shoot at the crowd of the poor and kill them,
Crush the thirst of a common man with heavy boots.

Be a messiah by provoking communal riots,
At every step, break trust in the human heart.

Throw a few slogans towards the common people,
Capture the month of spring in your living rooms.

---

[1] Genghis Khan (c. 1155/1162-1227) was the founder and Emperor of the Mongol Empire.

If half of the population burns in the flames of hunger

If half of the population burns in the flames of hunger,
Then how can a *ghazal* mature in the imagination of a poet?

Those who build the estimate of a dominant nation,
Their nights decline in a footpath's shade.

The innocent beauty of the village stands naked,
It is a matter of shame that these splendid fields sprout gold.

The elegance of a glorious nation are your palaces,
They will be burnt to ashes if the flowers of revolution blossom here.

How cynical has democracy become as it grows older,
At our heads the shadow of severity, and lips, sealed.

Hunger is an issue that, among people suffering from its wound

Hunger is an issue that, among people suffering from its wound,
So many a Yusuf[1] died without a shroud.

Bread became a target of beauty's innocence,
Under the shade in moonlight too, flowers feel like flames.

A mother's love, a father's eminence, have been consumed by rising expense,
As it happened divisions arose between two hearts.

The fragrance of love has vanished from traditional relationships,
The margins of life have soured with resentment.

The objective of life is this, keep fighting for your rights,
Suicide is not the destination, for those defeated by life.

---

[1] Yusuf (Joseph) was sold into slavery to Potiphar by his jealous brothers.

There is an awareness of the mechanical age in my poetry

There is an awareness of the mechanical age in my poetry,
The history of the nation burning in the fire of hunger.

How could it be extinguished by the dew of hollow slogans,
On energetic lips is thirst a whole century old.

What did Delhi[1] do for those nomads,
In winter who have the roof of an open sky over their head.

In lieu of a few coins, people are selling their conscience,
Is this our nation's parliament or a flesh market.

Civility has been burnt in the flames of the communal violence,
At the crossroads of art lies Draupadi's[2] naked corpse.

---

[1] India's political capital.

[2] The wife of the five Pandavas in the epic *Mahabharata*. After the game of dice, she was dragged by the hair to the court and is called a whore. The Kauravas make an attempt to disrobe her but she is miraculously protected by Lord Krishna.

There is only one speed from Tulsi to Rajendra

There is only one speed from Tulsi[1] to Rajendra,[2]
On the topic of sex, our mentality is sick.

That slim crest of millet,[3] that bud of jasmine,[4]
For the sake of her stomach, is ready to be sold on the streets.

Tell a writer, leave the women, write a story,
Observe which writer's vocation holds water.

There, woman is unholy, the prototype of sin,
Here, Shivmurti's Vimli[5] is like a noose around a neck.

Live through the reality of Maya Tyagi[6] someday,
Then write about the pleasures of enslavement, I will not stop you.

---

[1] Goswami Tulsidas (1497-1623) was a Ramanandi Vaishnava saint and poet, renowned for his epic *Ramcharitmanas*, a retelling of the Sanskrit Ramayana in Awadhi language.

[2] Rajendra Yadav (1929-2013) was a writer and a pioneer of the Hindi literary movement known as Nayi Kahani.

[3] Refers to a poem 'Kalgi bajare ki' ('Crest of millet') by Sachchidananda Hirananda Vatsyayan 'Agyeya' (1911-1987). 'Kalgi' is also a girl's name.

[4] Refers to a poem 'Juhi ki kali' ('The bud of jasmine') by Suryakant Tripathi 'Nirala' (1896-1961). 'Juhi' is also a girl's name.

[5] A character from the story 'Tiriya charitra' ('A woman's character') by Shivmurti's (1950-).

[6] Refers to Maya Tyagi rape case in Baghpat, Uttar Pradesh.

It is bribery, the black market, debauchery

It is bribery, the black market, debauchery,
Who is it that says there is corruption in India.

When all the villages were swept away in the floods of Ghagara,[1]
From that day onwards, there is a festive celebration in their bungalows.

From the day Baba Ramdev[2] became *Ardhnarishvara*,[3]
I often think, is it *yoga* or the trade of *yoga*.

Mister Anna Hazare[4] will you be able to do,
This city is made of glass and the government is stonehearted.

When politics has become the mistress of capitalists,
Common people have the open right to rebel.

---

[1] Ghaghara River is a major tributary of the River Ganges.
[2] Baba Ramdev is an influential yoga guru and co-founder the Patanjali Ayurved Ltd.
[3] The *Ardhanarishvara* (depicted as half-male and half-female) is a composite form of the Hindu deities Lord Shiva and Goddess Parvati.
[4] A social activist who has led movements to promote government transparency and fight corruption in public life.

Human beings have divided themselves into the camps of black and white

Human beings have divided themselves into the camps of black and white,
There are clothes of politics on the body of civilization.
For a piece of bread Dhaniya[1] sold her dignity,
Premchand's[2] Hori[3] is sad in Lamhi.[4]

On the body of the flower, the butterfly is changing sides.
Like a human being burning from hunger.
Your face is a bit foggy in my mind,
Like a tree drowned in a beautiful mist.

Just think, what did we achieve from independence,
Today, the crowd of common people is thirsty.
To hide your flaws, there is a blanket of Gandhi's philosophy,[5]
To get naked, there is Rajneesh's[6] *hammam*.[7]

Give the clothes of craft to these wild ideas,
Give them a mark to stay next the heart of time.

---

[1] Dhania is Hori's wife in Premachand's novel Godan (' The Gift of a Cow', 1936).

[2] Munshi Premchand (1880-1936), the pen name of Dhanpat Rai Srivastava, was a Hindi writer famous for his novels such as *Godaan*, *Karmabhoomi*, *Gaban*, *Mansarovar*, and *Idgah*.

[3] Hori is a peasant in Premachand's novel Godan (' The Gift of a Cow', 1936).

[4] The birthplace of Premchand, which is located north of Varanasi in Uttar Pradesh.

[5] Mohandas Karamchand Gandhi (1869-1948) was a lawyer and a non-violent anti-colonial nationalist who has inspired movements for civil rights and freedom across the world. *Gandhvaad* or Gandhi's philosophy is a body of ideas and values that describes the vision of Mahatma Gandhi.

[6] Bhagwan Shri Rajneesh (1931-1990), also known as Osho, was a mystic and founder of the Rajneesh movement.

[7] A Turkish bath.

Before asking how much youth there is in life.
To the poet carve up some sculpture.

Hesitant every glance; there are chains on every foot,
This is the portrait of my free Hindustan.
Many Alexanders[1] are buried in the dust of this country,
Mister thinks that it is his personal property.

---

[1] Alexander the Great was the king of Macedon who created an empire stretching from Greece to northwestern India.

This violence, this rioting, are a scene from the apocalypse

This violence, this rioting, are a scene from the apocalypse,
They say the reason behind this riot is a machine.
Mister, if you will look at it from my perspective,
Then a piece of bread is more beautiful than the moon.

Oh, fate! That the child fell asleep hungry,
Earlier, pacification, wrapped around the mother's feet.
What fault if his consciousness turns rebel,
His childhood is passing on the fire of hunger.

I lifted my hand with respect to salute,
They thought it was a threat to the system.
If we should not steal or lie, then what should we do,
Should we cook our principles for supper.

If a poet is distanced from the circle of life,
Then he is like a sore in the bosom of the civilization.
When tradition becomes iron chains round the feet,
Then human beings are compelled to rebel.

In the season of starvation they are writing verses of love,
Nowadays even poets are duplicitous in their behaviour.
Friends, in the name of democracy in this country,
For how long will we take orders from just one family?

Carrying a beautiful dream for a home in the eyes

Carrying a beautiful dream for a home in the eyes,
Life has been spent under the refuge of an old tree.
Give some air to the fire kindling in the heart,
Then see what power is in a poor man's moan.

He was not a soldier, neither trader nor labourer,
In reality, Munshi[1] was this era's Mansour.[2]
He gave a place to the common man in his tales,
When only tales of Alif Laila[3] were popular in this country.

Be it the pride of Socrates[4] or the life-story of Gandhi,[5]
Truth loses at the war-front of life.
Whenever you see someone walking past clad in torn clothes,
Understand this that path comes to Adam's[6] house.

During elections, we will exchange handkerchiefs with Muslims,
We have just changed our face; look, now we'll change our gait too.
Say defector, what difference does it make so long as we get the chair?
Is this parentage; we will switch political parties every year.

---

[1] Munshi Premchand (1880-1936) was a well-known modern Hindi writer.
[2] Mansour Hallaj (c. 858-922) was a Persian mystic, poet and teacher of Sufism.
[3] *Alif Layla wa-Layla* also known as *One Thousand and One Nights* or the *Arabian Nights*.
[4] Socrates (c. 470-399 BC) was a Greek philosopher and thinker. He was sentenced to death by drinking a mixture containing poison hemlock.
[5] Mohandas Karamchand Gandhi (1869-1948) was a lawyer and a non-violent anti-colonial nationalist who has inspired movements for civil rights and freedom across the world.
[6] Adam Gondvi.

Reasoning lights the flame of imagination in the unconscious mind,
At the level of natural sensibility, a poem takes birth.
Science lifts a foot in the darkness of doubt,
Suddenly, in that darkness, lightning flashes.

Adam,[1] this civilization has nothing to give anymore,
It just pisses on an agonized man.

[1] Adam Gondvi.

People have the right to bear arms and rebel

If leaders walk on the path of arrogance,
If leaders keep stooping low for their positions of power,
If leaders keep changing their colours like chameleons,
If leaders live off the money of black-marketers,
People have the right to bear arms and rebel.

When farmers are burning in the blaze of starvation,
When people with tongues are silent,
When the flames of rioting are young in the season of hatred,
When on the body of democracy there are signs of rape,
People have the right to bear arms and rebel.

If someone thinks of himself as the fate of a nation,
If someone thinks of all things as an interpretation of his dreams,
If someone thinks of his statements as the composition of *Vedas*,[1]
If someone thinks of the populace as his family's property,
People have the right to bear arms and rebel.

It is the country of Gandhi[2] but the situation is absurd,
Bureaucrats are corrupt and doctors are executioners,
People are not even fortunate enough to drink clean water,
After drinking rum, artists and poets wag their tails like dogs,
People have the right to bear arms and rebel.

---

[1] The four key texts of Hinduism: the Rigveda, the Yajurveda, the Samaveda and the Atharvaveda.

[2] Mohandas Karamchand Gandhi (1869-1948) was a lawyer and a non-violent anti-colonial nationalist who has inspired movements for civil rights and freedom across the world.

PS:
Boil a few eggs,
Bring out a bottle of wine,
They will come to your home too,
Keep your family inside all the time.

Let me stitch natural beauty in the celestial orbit of words

Let me stitch natural beauty in the celestial orbit of words,
Let me engrave the reflection of my beloved's charming face in poetry.

Let me mix the fragrance of a passionate kiss in poetry,
Let me open that window that will unveil beauty.

Let me take you to the gala of *Gopis*[1] suffering from separation,
Let me present the world of Bhasa[2] and Kalidasa.[3]

But my village's atmosphere is cursed,
Common people are suffering in the heat of starvation.

Those who are strong, both religion and administration are with him,
Poor people's wealth is their two hands.

Does any holy scripture mention that oppression is a sin,
That is why I say that religion is hypocrisy and a curse.

Every young man assembles his dreams with longing,
But is he able to fulfil them with the same fervour,

He wishes for his own house and a village of his own,
He wishes for the dense shade of his beloved's open hair.

---

1 Refer to the group of cowherding girls or milkmaids known for their unconditional devotion to Lord Krishna.

2 Bhasa was an early Sanskrit playwright.

3 Kalidasa was a Classical Sanskrit playwright and dramatist.

After a full day's work, he will return tired,
Spread on the threshold in welcome, brimming innocent eyes.

Alas, fate! Unfortunately, here dreams turn sour,
Because of starvation, even flowers become flames.

Helplessness mixes poison in the goblet of life,
In a moment the palace of our dreams is shattered.

His boat falters in the storm of creation,
When unsuccessful he blames it on fate and God.

Where half of the population is suffering from hunger,
Common people are afraid, disturbed and penniless.

Will they be ethical? How is this even possible?
How can a firefly light the moonless night?

Those who have been mounted on the peak of success,
In their eyes the poor are obnoxious and illiterate.

They themselves are distanced from hard work but still wealthy and rich,
They are fewer in number but strong from fraud and deceit.

They play with the bud and smile of the flower,
They snatch away others' rights with the arrogance of their caste.

Will the blast of rebellion ever take place among the poor,
Will the flaws be exposed among the common people.

Deep-rooted the notion that of whoever is miserable in this birth,
Of whoever is suffering in the heat of starvation and poor,

Only those who live with austerity will receive happiness in heaven,
And those who are aberrant will burn in the fires of hell.

An explanation like this is an amazing trick to keep people under an illusion,
Worse than hell is our country's each village.

Your religion and these tales of unending afterlife,
A plot with destiny and the worship of imaginary gods.

Today, the curtain is lifting from mass shame and ignorance,
Even your gods are horrified before science.

The bitterness of sentiments gives the feel of a new era,
At every step, it breaks and scatters the garland of trust.

Under the dense shade of mango trees on the banks of rivers,
There is a discussion in the world that India lives in villages.

Come and let us perform some introspection by this statement,
Shouldn't we first survey the alleyways of our village?

Look at that palace standing upright with pride,
Standing like the moon taking birth from the womb of the night.

That old gentleman who is praying outside the door,
He is a cunning fellow, has been collecting money treacherously.

He is exploiting by taking interest on the loan, think of him as a thief.
Being sagacious is his ruse, he is in reality an anthropophagi.

To pretend, he is a devotee of Lord Hanuman,[1]
His god is expressed eloquently in the jingling of coins.

At present, he is reading *Gita*[2] but his mind is thinking tricks,
No one knows how many homes have been destroyed under the shade of his sagaciousness.

For the public, he has kept her in his home his little sister,
No one knows how many Draupadis[3] have lost their dignity at his hand.

How many Dushasana[4] are still in this village of our nation?
Wolves rule under the guise of sages here.

Each man of the village is merely a vote for them,
Only in name have we democracy; otherwise, every election is an attack.

As we lost the blood of our loved ones, India gained freedom,
As for inheritance, we got communal violence and destruction,

The distance between the bungalows and huts,
The helplessness of the man struggling under starvation.

---

[1] A Hindu god (monkey) and a companion of the Lord Rama in the epic *Ramayana*.

[2] The Bhagavad Gita ('The Song of God') is a 700-verse Hindu scripture that is part of the epic *Mahabharata* (chapters 23-40 of Bhishma Parva).

[3] The wife of the five Pandavas in the epic *Mahabharata*. After the game of dice, she was dragged by the hair to the court and is called a whore. The Kauravas make an attempt to disrobe her but she is miraculously protected by Lord Krishna.

[4] Dushasana was a Kaurava prince and the younger brother of Duryodhana in the Hindu epic *Mahabharata*. After the game of dice, he dragged Draupadi by the hair into the assembly and tried to disrobe her.

Is there no solution; should we fill in the gulf,
Should we distribute the pain of the man amongst others.

I will take you to the colony of the Chamars

Come and feel the intense heat of life,
I will take you to the colony of the *Chamars*.[1]

In that alley where sick of the torture of starvation,
Poor Phuliya died yesterday, drowned in a well.

Carrying on an upright head a basket of twigs,
Approaching straight ahead is Harkhua's girl.

She is walking providing direction to the dimension of a couplet,
I call her Mona Lisa[2] across the Sarayu.[3]

How terrified she is – afraid as a hind,
Looks like a wilted bud on a vine.

Yesterday a blabbermouth but today she is a mute,
Do you know who the reason behind her silence is.

One of these monsoon days Harkhu went to the market,
The old woman was sleeping on a cot stretched on the porch.

The rays of the setting sun were playing with the sand,
She was returning from the fields carrying bales of grass.

She was walking along quite lost in some feeling,

---

[1] An untouchable caste. The term is used as a pejorative word for *Dalits* in general in India.
[2] The Mona Lisa is a well-known half-length portrait painting by the Italian artist Leonardo da Vinci.
[3] A river that originates in Uttarakhand and flows through Uttar Pradesh.

Little did she know that a wolf lay in wait.

Unaware of doom Krishnaa walked her unwary path,
Turned with the road and found herself in aliens arms.

If she screamed the sound was stifled within,
She struggled at first, then went limp, then dimmed.

The day trapped in Sarayu's bowls had long since set.
Her girlhood was burnt in the fires of prurience.

And that day this manor house laughed in sportive play,
Regaining consciousness Krishnaa was in her father's embrace.

A crowd had gathered, with all the vigor of a flood,
Whoever was there was keen to have his say.

Advancing Mangal said Uncle, how are you mute,
Ask your daughter, after all, who the monster is.

We will not turn our feet away from any striving now,
We will tear him apart, we will not let him live.

How can we call it happenstance again and once more let it pass
And with our brides and daughters these foes glut mouths full of blackened blood.

He said to Krishnaa sister, sleep now by my appeal,
That sinner won't be spared of my stern vengeance is my vow.

Word reached the ears of Thakurs[1] in the village,

---

[1] An upper caste. A feudal title used by erstwhile nobility or landlords.

They gathered in the courtyard of the chieftain.

Sights firmly set at the edge of the spear's blade,
Look Sukhraj Singh speaks, spitting out his piece[1].

What can one say chief! What times have come,
Those underfoot till yesterday have acquired status too.

The government tells us to live in harmony with each other,
Don't call these sons of pigs *Kori*[2] but *Harijan*[3] now on.

See, this Krishnaa in the house of the *Chamars*,
A pearl has fallen to the colony of illiterates.

Like the monsoon river sloshing about artless drunk,
She does not permit the hand on her hip, she is arrogant.

Harkhua does not even send her away, off to a married home,
If someone hooked her into his arms, what happened, so?

Today, she ran into our Shyam across the Sarayu,
Knowing unknowingly, she found the savor of life.

It was Mangal who saw to it the matter got on,
Otherwise, far be it for that outcast to talk.

You all know that Mangal alone is the sneak,
Harkhu is ready at his say to go to the police.

If tomorrow morning my son and I are snagged,

---

[1] Chewing tobacco.

[2] A lower caste of weavers.

[3] Mahatma Gandhi (1869-1948) coined the word *Harijan* (people of God) in 1933 to identify dalits and untouchables.

What deference will be left for you in the village streets?

The accent was such it excited everyone's ire,
As is usual (in such spaces) hands rose to moustaches.

The momentary fury in which every youth was Taimur,[1]
Oh yes, but fate has something else in mind.

The storm that didn't come at night was in full strength now,
At dawn, the scene there had completely changed.

With caps on their heads and batons in their hands,
A dozen policemen, with the Thakurs, approached in a band.

Surrounding the colony, the inspector said softly:
The man known as Mangal should come forward now.

Opening the door slightly Mangal emerged from his hut,
A policeman weighed the moment and brought his baton down.

As Mangal fell a boot advanced, rose and kicked,
Talk, you bastard, what you did with the loot from the hit.

What hit? What loot? He seemed to say,
Another policeman hit him and his senses slipped away.

Blacked out he lay upon the threshold of his hut,
The inspector hollered to the Thakurs in challenge and ridicule –

Why do you stand there looking at my face? Come spit on him,

---

[1] Taimur Lang or Tamerlane (1336-1405) was a Turco-Mongol conqueror who founded the Timurid Empire in and around modern-day Afghanistan, Iran and Central Asia.

Bring the fire, smoke his place.

And then the storm of vengeance began there to blow,
The home of the unprotected, the weak began to burn.

The infants and the elderly present that day there,
Those unfortunate wretches were in the clutches of a murderous mob.

Seeing their home burning they were apt to lose their mind,
Some sat there silently, and some began to wail.

Tell these sons of bitches not to fret,
Until I give the order, no one goes anywhere.

This was the inspector showering words like flowers,
Walking on and shoving people with his mighty rule.

He then roared they will be schooled with cudgels this day,
Whoever clashes with the Thakurs will be obliterated.

A policeman asked where to turn the bicycle now,
Mangal still unconscious, shall we leave him this way.

The inspector answered do not crow like a timorous cock,
If he is not conscious swing his body onto sticks.

These folks think it is a game to tangle with the Thakur,
The place for such bastards is not at home but in a jail.

People often ask me this question alone,
Tell, won't you, how Krishnaa is, from Sarayu's beyond

To their excitement, to the city's fever for nakedness,
To the decomposing republic's dodgy administrators,

To the caretakers of religion, culture and morality,
To the state's ministers and the central government,

I extend an invitation, please come to my village,
Under the shade of mango trees on the banks of rivers,

Villages, where today Panchali[1] is being stripped,
Or where non-violence is being raped.

There are so many many Mangals groaning for a loincloth,
There are many a Krishnaas selling their bodies for a piece of bread.

[1] Draupadi who was the daughter of the King of Panchal Dhrupada.